I Am the Artist!

Written by Dawn Anderson
Illustrated by Kelley Cunningham

Children's Press®
A Division of Scholastic Inc.
New York • Toronto • London • Auckland • Sydney
Mexico City • New Delhi • Hong Kong
Danbury, Connecticut

To my parents Donald and Dolores,
and to my husband Michael
—D.A.

For my sons Sam, Noah, and Nathaniel
—K.C.

Reading Consultant

Eileen Robinson
Reading Specialist

3 9082 10256 1480

Library of Congress Cataloging-in-Publication Data

Anderson, Dawn, 1977-
  I am the artist! / written by Dawn Anderson ; illustrated by Kelley Cunningham.
      p. cm. — (A rookie reader)
  Summary: A young boy has fun creating a painting with a variety of colors.
  ISBN 0-516-24976-2 (lib. bdg.)   0-516-24912-6 (pbk.)
  [1. Painting—Fiction. 2. Color—Fiction.] I. Cunningham, Kelley, 1963- ill. II. Title. III. Series.
  PZ7.A533124Iaam 2006
  [E]—dc22

                            2005016128

My little sister paints.

I think it's silly.
She gets all messy.

Paint is in her hair
and on the cat!

She looks like she
is having fun.

9

Maybe I'll give it a try.
I pick up a brush.

I paint a sky.
I make it blue.

I paint a sun.
I make it yellow.

I paint a cloud.
I make it white.

I paint a tree.
I make it green.

I paint an apple.
I make it red.

I paint a rock.
I make it brown.

I paint a flower.
I make it orange.

I paint a lion.
I make it purple.

"Lions aren't purple!"
says my sister.

"I am the artist!" I say.

Word List (58 Words)

(Words in **bold** are story words that are repeated throughout the text.)

a	her	pick
all	**I**	purple
am	I'll	red
an	in	rock
and	is	say
apple	**it**	says
aren't	it's	she
artist	like	silly
blue	lion	sister
brown	lions	sky
brush	little	sun
cat	looks	the
cloud	**make**	think
flower	maybe	tree
fun	messy	try
gets	my	up
give	on	white
green	orange	yellow
hair	**paint**	
having	paints	

About the Author

Dawn Anderson has been writing stories since she was a young girl. She lives in Overland Park, Kansas, with her husband, Mike, their dog, and two cats. When she is not writing stories, Dawn likes to be an artist herself.

About the Illustrator

Kelley Cunningham always wanted to be an artist and began drawing when she was a young girl. She's very happy to be getting paid to do something she loves. Born in Wisconsin, Kelley now lives in New Jersey with her husband and three sons.